SCOOBY SNACKS
Recipe Book

CONTENTS

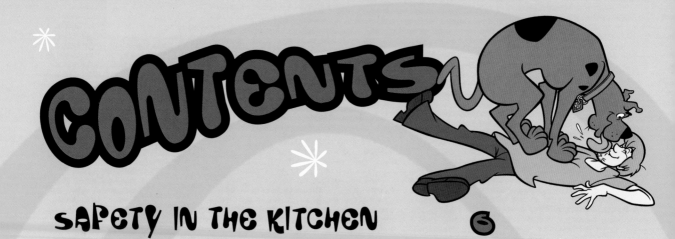

SAFETY IN THE KITCHEN

1 Do not attempt any of these recipes without an adult with you. Ovens are hot, and knives are sharp. If you do cut or burn yourself, place the wound under cold running water and call for help.

2 Wash and dry your hands thoroughly and put on an apron before starting to cook.

3 Make sure your work area is clean and tidy. Clean up dishes and utensils as you go – it will give you more time to enjoy your efforts.

4 Before you start, read each recipe all the way through. You should make sure you understand everything you need to do, and have everything you need. Familiarize yourself with kitchen equipment such as chopping boards and electric mixers.

5 Measure out all your ingredients carefully using plastic or glass measuring cups and spoons.

6 Never leave the kitchen when the electric or gas rings are still on.

7 Always make sure you have turned off the oven when you have finished.

GROOVY PARTY SNACKS

Have your own groovy Scooby party with these fun snacks — your friends will love them!

SWEET POPCORN

Personalize your friends' popcorn at your movie marathons with these Mystery Inc. cocktail decorations.

EQUIPMENT

| sticky tape | 6 cocktail sticks | wooden spoon | saucepan with lid | cups or glasses | tablespoon |

INGREDIENTS   (makes 5–6 cups/glasses)

   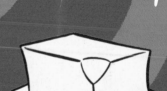

| 100g popping corn | 2 tablespoons sunflower oil | 6 tablespoons maple syrup | 50g butter |

8

1 Begin by making the cocktail-stick decorations. Colour photocopy the head shots of the Mystery Inc. gang, enlarging as needed. Cut out and sticky tape them to the blunt end of the cocktail sticks. Put the sticks to one side.

2 Empty the oil into a large saucepan, add one layer of corn kernels, and put on the lid. Place over a medium heat.

3 You will begin to hear the kernels popping. With the lid still firmly on, shake the saucepan a few times to encourage all the kernels to pop.

4 Empty the oil into a large saucepan, add one layer of corn kernels, and put on the lid. Place over a medium heat.

5 Once it has finished popping, remove from the heat and carefully look inside. If there are still any popcorn kernels left unpopped, place back on the heat and repeat previous steps.

6 Add the maple syrup and butter, stirring well with a wooden spoon.

7 Fill coloured cups or glasses with hot, sticky popcorn.

8 Add one cocktail stick per glass.

TIP For savoury popcorn, just leave out the maple syrup and add a sprinkling of salt and a little butter.

When is a rooster like Scooby?

When it acts chicken!

9

SNACKS-ON-A-STICK

EQUIPMENT

You can put whatever you want on bamboo skewers – make them sweet or savoury! Use fruit, cooked meat, vegetables or sweets.

chopping board

chopping knife

long bamboo skewers

INGREDIENTS

Some ideas for the snacks.

basil leaves

Cheddar cheese

asparagus

pitted olives

peppers

cherry tomatoes

salami slices

prawns

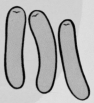

mini hot dogs

clementine or mandarin segments

strawberries

marshmallows

kiwis

chewy sweets

TIP Savoury skewers go well with salsa and dips, whereas sweet kebabs go well with yoghurt.

1 It's important to decide what sort of flavours will work together – don't mix sweet foods with savoury! Cheese works well with meat and vegetables, while fruit taste good on its own or with sweets.

2 Chop all the foods into chunks.

3 Pierce your foods on to the skewers, alternating between each different food type.

Here are some yummy combinations:
- Prawns, asparagus, tomato
- Mini-hot dogs and peppers
- Salami, olives, cheese, peppers
- Basil, cheese, tomato
- Strawberry, kiwi fruit, marshmallow
- Clementine segments, chewy sweets, kiwi fruit

Scooby's combinations:
(these aren't so yummy!)
- Furballs, steak chunks, whole garlic cloves
- Scooby snacks, houseflies, red-hot chillies
- Beetroot, ice-cream scoops, pork chops
- Apple, pickled onions, sardines, banana

How come the Cheese Phantom is so hard to spot on a hot day?

Because he just melts into the background!

BAT MINI-PIZZAS

The great thing about making these pizzas is that you can arrange your favourite toppings to look like monsters, witches or whatever spooks you most!

EQUIPMENT

chopping board and knife

sieve

bowl

wooden spoon

sharp knife

rolling pin

baking tray

rolling pin

INGREDIENTS

FOR THE PIZZA BASES

150g self-raising flour

40g butter or margarine

3–4 tablespoons milk

50g grated Cheddar cheese

FOR THE SAUCE

1 dessertspoon tomato puree

1 small tin tomatoes

1 small onion

pinch of salt

pinch of pepper

50g grated cheese

2 slices gammon or thick ham

1 small tin sweetcorn

1 stick pepperoni

Sliced green peppers

MAKING THE SAUCE

TIP

Wearing goggles when chopping up onions will stop your eyes from stinging.

1 Peel the onion, cut it in half and chop finely on a chopping board.

2 Place the onion in a small saucepan. Add the tomatoes, tomato puree and a pinch of salt and pepper.

3 Cook over a low heat for 15 minutes, stirring a few times. Take the pan off the heat and let the mixture cool.

LIFE-SIZE BAT TEMPLATE

13

MAKING THE DOUGH

You can make the dough while the sauce is cooking.
But don't forget to stir the sauce every now and then!

1 Set the oven to 220°C/425°F/gas mark 7.

2 Cut the butter or margarine into small pieces, and put it into the mixing bowl. Add the salt.

3 Sift the flour into the bowl.

4 Using your fingertips, 'rub' small pieces of the butter or margarine into the flour until the mix looks like breadcrumbs. Remember to make a 'rubbing' motion using just the tips of your fingers, or the butter or margarine will melt.

5 Add the milk and grated cheese. Mix everything with a wooden spoon until you have a ball of dough.

6 Divide the dough into two, and make each into a round ball. Using a rolling pin, roll each ball of dough into a circle about 10 cm across. Flour the surface first or they will stick.

7 Grease a baking tray and lay out the dough circles. Spoon a layer of tomato sauce on top of them, spreading it out evenly to the edges.

DECORATING THE PIZZA

1. Sprinkle the grated cheese over the pizzas.

2. Trace the bat template on page 13 to greaseproof paper, and cut it out. Place the paper on the gammon or ham, and cut round it carefully with a sharp knife. Place the bat in the centre of the pizza.

3. Take two sweetcorn kernels and place on top of the bat for eyes.

4. Slice peppers finely and sprinkle around the edge of the pizza.

5. Slice the pepperoni finely and arrange in a ring around the outside of the pizza.

6. Cook the pizzas in the oven for 15–20 minutes, until the edges have browned.

When is a tap like Scooby and Shaggy?

When it's running!

CHEESY TWISTS

WARNING!
Never use a sharp knife without an adult present.

These cheese straws are surprisingly easy to make, and they taste great. Serve with a range of dips.

EQUIPMENT

sieve

bowl

wooden spoon

rolling pin

ruler

sharp knife

baking tray

teaspoon

INGREDIENTS

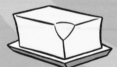

100g butter or margarine

200g plain flour

75g grated Cheddar cheese

2 teaspoons water

1 egg yolk

1 pinch cayenne pepper

1 pinch salt

1 Pre-heat the oven to 180°C/350°F/gas mark 4.

2 Using a sieve, sift the flour into the bowl.
As described in the previous recipe, 'rub' in the butter or margarine with the tips of your fingers.

3 Add the cheese and the cayenne pepper to the bowl and, with a wooden spoon, stir the ingredients well.

4 Add egg yolk and cold water, stirring until the mixture becomes a soft dough.
Using your hands, knead the dough until the mixture is of a smooth consistency.

5 Sprinkle flour on to a chopping board or a dry, clean, work surface.
Using a rolling pin, roll out the dough evenly to about ½ cm thickness.

6 Using a ruler and sharp knife, cut the dough into thin strips about 6 cm long. 'Twist' each strip once in the middle.

7 Flour a baking tray and transfer the cheese strips.
(The flour absorbs the fat from the cheese as it melts.)

8 Pop the tray in the oven and bake for 5–6 minutes.

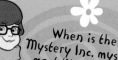

When is the Mystery Inc. mystery most like an egg?
When we crack it!

TIP Make sure you watch these when cooking, as they burn easily.

GHOULISH MILKSHAKES

WARNING!
Do not use your blender without adult supervision.

They may look strange, but these thick, creamy supershakes are packed with good things like fruit, honey and natural yoghurt.

EQUIPMENT

blender

glass

tablespoon

INGREDIENTS

1 tablespoon of vanilla ice cream

150mls milk

1 tablespoon honey

3 tablespoons of natural yoghurt

FOR A GREEN SUPERSHAKE

Scoop out the insides of 2–3 kiwi fruits

FOR A PURPLE MILKSHAKE

Add 75g of blueberries

18

1 Put all the ingredients in the blender, including the fruit. Place the lid on firmly and whiz until you have a lovely frothy supershake.

2 Pour into a large glass and serve.

TIP

Add a couple of drops of purple or green food colouring to make your shakes even more ghoulishly-coloured.

Food Colouring

TIP

You can make the Mystery Inc. gang cocktail sticks on page 8 and garnish with fruit.

Why did the milk shake?

Ry?

Because it heard the ice cream!

GHOSTLY MERINGUES

Meringues take a long time to cook — so make sure you start this one early!

EQUIPMENT

greaseproof paper

bowl

cup

baking tray

whisk

tablespoon

teaspoon

INGREDIENTS

2 eggs

100g caster sugar

glacé cherries or currants

1 pinch salt

1. Set oven on to its lowest setting. Take a baking tray, and cut a piece of greaseproof baking paper to fit it.

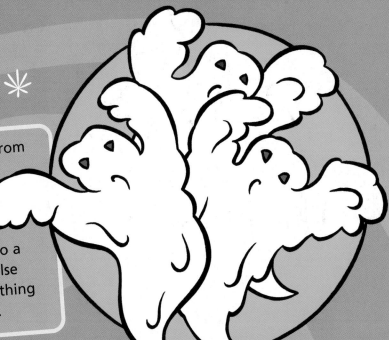

2. You need to separate the egg whites from their yolks. Carefully crack one egg in half over a bowl, and pour the yolk into the other shell. Repeat until all the white has fallen out into the bowl below. Put the yolk into a cup and set aside – you or someone else may be able to use this to cook something else later. Repeat with the other egg.

3. Add your pinch of salt to the egg whites and beat with a whisk until they turn from clear and runny to white and stiff. They should form peaks when you lift the whisk out.

4. Gradually add the sugar to the mixture, whisking until the mixture looks shiny.

5. Using a heaped tablespoon, shape a meringue on the baking tray. Using the back of the teaspoon, make a hollow in the mixture. Heap spoonfuls of meringue on to the hollowed base, using the teaspoon to spread the mixture out into a ghost shape (similar to the picture). Repeat for other meringues.

6. Cut pieces of glacé cherry or use currants for eyes and put them on the meringues.

What did Scooby say when he sat on the grater?

Ruff!

7. Place the baking tray in the oven and bake slowly for 4–5 hours. When the meringues are set, place them on a cooling rack.

SCOOBY CAKE

You can use all sorts of cake recipes for this Scooby Cake, including chocolate. Here, we have just used a simple sponge cake.

EQUIPMENT

cake tin
2 x 18cm

greaseproof paper

pencil

scissors

butter knife

wooden spoon

fork

big spoon

spatula

small saucepan

sieve

mug

cooling tray

INGREDIENTS

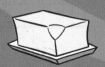
175g butter
(at room temperature)
Small amount of butter
for greasing the cake tins

175g caster sugar

175g self-raising flour

3 large eggs

22

FOR THE ICING

150g icing sugar

2 tablespoons cocoa powder

1 1/2 tablespoons butter

1 1/2 tablespoons cream cheese

1/4 teaspoon vanilla essence

4 tablespoons boiling water

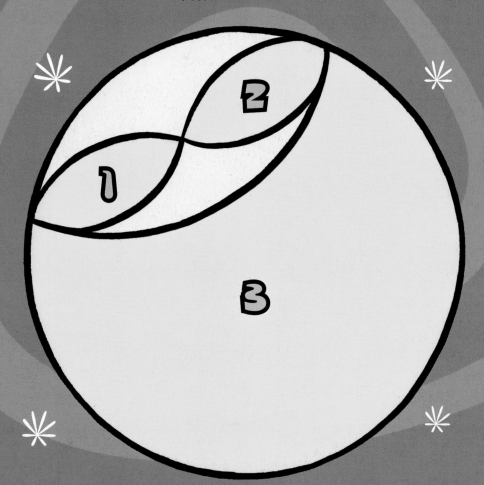

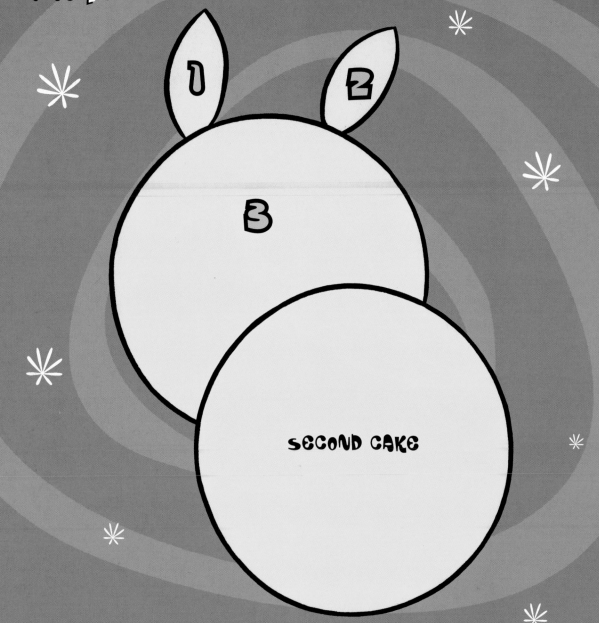

1 Pre-heat the oven to 180°C/350°F/gas mark 4.

2 Place a cake tin on the baking paper, draw a circle round it with a pencil. Using scissors, cut the circle out. Repeat for the other tin.

3 Lightly grease the inside of the tins with a small amount of butter. Place the circles of paper inside each tin and set aside.

4 In a large mixing bowl, place the sugar and butter. With a knife, chop the butter into chunks. Beat the sugar and butter with a wooden spoon or an electric mixer, until the mixture is light and fluffy.

5 Break an egg into a mug and beat with a fork. Then, a tiny bit at a time, add the egg to the creamed mixture, mixing well. Do the same with the remaining eggs.

6 Place a sieve over the bowl and sift half the flour over the mixture. Using a large metal spoon, gently mix the flour in thoroughly with a 'folding' motion. This is important, as you want as much air as possible inside the mixture to make it light and fluffy. Repeat with the remaining flour.

7 Pour half the cake mixture into each of the tins. Place both tins in the centre of the oven for 20–25 minutes.

8 You know when the cakes are cooked if the sides have shrunk away from the sides of the tin, and the top is golden. Take the cakes out of the oven and let them cool for a few minutes. Run a blunt knife around the outside of the cakes, and tip them out on to a cooling rack. Carefully remove the baking paper. Leave cakes to cool.

9 The template of Scooby (on page 23 and opposite) shows you how to assemble the Scooby cake. Cut them out and place together on a plate as shown.

MAKING THE ICING

1 Put a small saucepan on the hob and add the butter and cream cheese. Stir with a wooden spoon and mix until melted. Take the pan off the heat.

2 Mix the cocoa powder and icing sugar together. Pour the butter mixture into the bowl and mix with an electric mixer until it becomes all crumbly. Add the vanilla. Then slowly add the hot water and mix on high speed until the mixture is smooth and runny.

3 Using a spatula, cover the cake with icing. Decorate with large white chocolate buttons for eyes, with round black wine gums for the pupils. Use a large red gummy sweet or ribbon for his tongue, and a chocolate biscuit for his nose. Use two large black jellybeans for eyebrows.

FINISHED CAKE

What do the Maple Syrup Monsters do in a crisis?
They stick together!

26

REALLY BIG SNACKS

These snacks are perfect for those after-school munchies – and taste even better if you share them with a friend! But keep an eye on your plate – they just might disappear!

NOTSO HOTSO HOT DOG

Hot dogs are quick and tasty. This recipe tastes just as good if you leave out the chilli sauce.

EQUIPMENT

chopping board and knife

sieve

big pan

tongs

tablespoon

INGREDIENTS

For four hot dogs.

1/4 onion

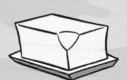
1 tablespoon butter

ketchup

chilli sauce (optional)

50 grams grated cheese

4 white bread hot-dog buns

4 frankfurter sausages

Put a big pan of water on the stove, cover with a lid and boil.

 Add the sausages and boil for 5 minutes (or according to the instructions on the package).

 While the sausages are heating up, chop up the onion finely. Heat the butter in a saucepan, and once it has melted, add the onion. Stir and fry onions until they are brown, and take off the heat.

 On a chopping board, slice the hot-dog buns in half with a bread knife.

 Drain the frankfurters in a sieve. Using tongs, place one hot dog inside each of the buns.

Top with onion, ketchup, grated cheese, and chilli sauce for a bit of extra zing!

When is Scooby like a hot dog?

Like, on a hot summer's day, man!

THE SUPER-DOOPER SANDWICH

This sandwich can really fill that gaping hole in your stomach – just pile on your favourite fillings.

EQUIPMENT

plate

butter knife

chopping board and knife

WARNING!
Never use a sharp knife without an adult present.

INGREDIENTS

3 slices bread

sliced ham or other cooked meats

cheese slices

bag of prepared salad

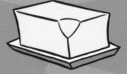

butter or margarine

small jar sliced beetroot

1 tomato

chilli sauce and mustard (optional)

The great thing about this sandwich is you can stack it as high as you like. If you like things hot, add some chilli sauce or mustard. If you aren't sure, try a tiny, tiny amount first!

1 Butter or margarine one side of two slices of bread, putting the third to one side.

2 Place the ham on top of the buttered bread slices.

3 Put a layer of moist fillings on the meat slices, such as the tomato on one and the beetroot on the other.
This separates it from the bread and stops it from going soggy.

4 Place a thin layer of lettuce on each sandwich stack, followed by the sliced cheese.
Add mustard and a touch of chilli if you dare!

5 Very carefully, lift up one of the sandwich piles and place on top of the other.

6 Top off the sandwich with the third slice of bread. Present on a plate and get snacking!

What's the only kind of witch that I like?

A multi-decker marine sand-witch!

31

MONSTROUSLY GOOD SPICY NACHOS

SUPER SNACK!

These are fun to make and really fill you up. Perfect to share in front of a scary movie!

WARNING! Never use a sharp knife without an adult present.

EQUIPMENT

sieve   teaspoon   measuring jug

chopping board and knife   potato peeler   garlic crusher   wooden spoon   tablespoon   small pan with lid   large saucepan   shallow oven-proof dish

INGREDIENTS

500g extra lean minced beef   1 onion   2 carrots   2 garlic cloves   1 tablespoon olive oil   1 teaspoon ground cumin

200ml chicken or beef stock   salt & pepper   400g tin chopped tomatoes   400g tin kidney beans   2 teaspoons paprika

TOPPINGS

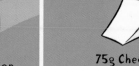

75g Cheddar or mozzarella cheese

125g frozen mixed vegetables   125g tortilla chips

1. Peel and chop the onion in half on the chopping board. Dice finely.

2. Using a vegetable peeler, peel the carrot, then chop into small squares.

3. Peel the cloves of garlic, and crush in a garlic crusher.

4. Heat the oil in a large saucepan and add the onion, garlic, carrots and mince. Stir with a wooden spoon, until the mince is evenly browned.

5. Add the paprika, cumin, beans, chopped tomatoes, the stock and a pinch of salt and pepper.

6. Break up any large pieces of mince with the spoon and stir. Bring the mixture to the boil, and cover and cook gently for 45 minutes. Stir it every now and then to prevent it from sticking.

7. Fill a smaller saucepan with water and the frozen vegetables. Cover and bring to the boil, cooking for 4 minutes. Drain using the sieve.

8. Turn on the grill. Transfer the mince into a shallow ovenproof dish. Spoon the vegetable over the top and cover with tortilla chips. Grate cheese and sprinkle it over the chips, and grill until the cheese bubbles. It is now ready to serve.

TIP

Wearing goggles when chopping up onions will stop your eyes from stinging.

What's Shaggy's favourite fast food?

Terri-fried chicken!

EYEBALLS AND SPOOKHETTI

This ghoulish dish is not only a feast for the eyes, it makes a very tasty meal.

EQUIPMENT

mixing bowl

large baking dish

big pan

colander

big spoon

teaspoon

INGREDIENTS serves 4–5 people

1 large jar spaghetti sauce

500g extra lean minced beef

1 teaspoon olive oil

1 small jar green olives, stuffed with pimentos

Pinch of garlic salt
(just use salt if you don't like garlic)

1 teaspoon oregano

3 teaspoons breadcrumbs

1 egg

250g spaghetti

pinch of salt and pepper

34

MAKING THE EYEBALLS

1 Preheat the oven to 180°C/350°F/gas mark 4.

2 Get a large mixing bowl and a large spoon. Place the mince, the oregano, the breadcrumbs and a sprinkling of salt and pepper into the bowl. Crack the egg into the bowl, and mix the contents thoroughly. (The egg will make the mixture stick together.)

3 Use a tablespoon to spoon out the mixture. Use your hands to mould the meat mixture into a 2–3 cm-sized meatball.

4 Take one of the olives, and push into the meatball, making sure that the pimento is showing. Place your 'eyeball' on to a large baking dish. Repeat with the rest of the mixture.

5 Pour the jar of sauce over the meatballs. Place the tray in the centre of the oven and cook for 1 hour.

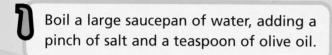

MAKING THE SPOOKHETTI

1 Boil a large saucepan of water, adding a pinch of salt and a teaspoon of olive oil.

2 Cook the spaghetti according to the instructions on the packet.

3 When cooked, strain through a colander.

4 Serve spookhetti with the eyeballs, spooning the sauce over the mixture.

What are two things Shaggy and Scooby can't eat for breakfast?

Lunch and dinner!

MEGA-GROOVY SPUDS

SUPER SNACK!

This tasty snack is very filling and makes a great light meal – perfect to fuel a hard afternoon's mystery-solving!

EQUIPMENT

bowl

baking tray

butter knife

fork

spoon

INGREDIENTS (for one person)

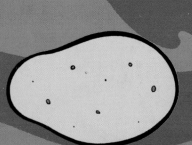
1 large baking potato

3 tablespoons baked beans

50g grated cheese

2 or 3 chopped pickled onions

1 tablespoon ketchup

You can use as little or a much of the fillings as you like – this is just a guide. You could also try this with tuna, sweetcorn and mayonnaise.

1. Preheat the oven to 190°C /375°F/gas mark 5.

2. Using a fork, prick the potato a couple of times. This will stop it bursting from its skin. Put on a baking tray and cook for one and a half hours. Prick with a fork to see if it is cooked. If not, leave it in for another 10 minutes or so.

3. Cut the potato in half and scoop out the middle into a bowl and mix with the baked beans, onions, cheese and the ketchup. Put the filling back inside the potato and bake for another fifteen minutes. Serve with a side salad.

Zoinks! Like, where did that vampire go?

I think he just popped out for a bite.

SWEET 'N' TASTY SNACKS

Brighten up your lunchbox or dessert-time with these delicious snacks, which none of the gang can resist!

SCOOBY SNACKS

Shaggy and Scooby can never, ever get enough of these cookies – soon you won't be able to either!

EQUIPMENT

 bowl

 baking tray

 sieve

 saucepan

 mug

 wooden spoon

 tablespoon

teaspoons

INGREDIENTS Makes about 35 cookies

 125g plain flour

 250g sugar

 125g rolled oats

 100g dessicated coconut

 1 tablespoon boiling water

 2 tablespoons golden syrup

 1/2 teaspoon bicarbonate of soda

 125g butter

40

1 Preheat oven to 150°C/300°F/gas mark 2.

2 Lightly grease two large baking trays.

3 Place the sifted flour, oats, sugar and coconut into a large mixing bowl and mix together with a wooden spoon.

4 Put the butter and golden syrup into a small saucepan and place on a low heat. Stir continuously with a clean wooden spoon until the butter has melted. Take off the heat.

5 Place the bicarbonate of soda and the water in a mug, and stir with a teaspoon. Add the contents of the mug to the golden syrup mixture, stirring well and then add to the dry ingredients in the mixing bowl. Using the wooden spoon, stir well until the mixture sticks together to form a dough.

6 Using a teaspoon, take a spoonful of the mixture and drop on to the tray. You may need to use the back of the spoon to spread the mixture out slightly. Repeat for each cookie. Make sure you leave at least 3 cm in between each cookie, as they will spread as they cook.

7 Place in the pre-heated oven for about 20 minutes.

8 Take the cookies out and allow them to cool on a wire rack.

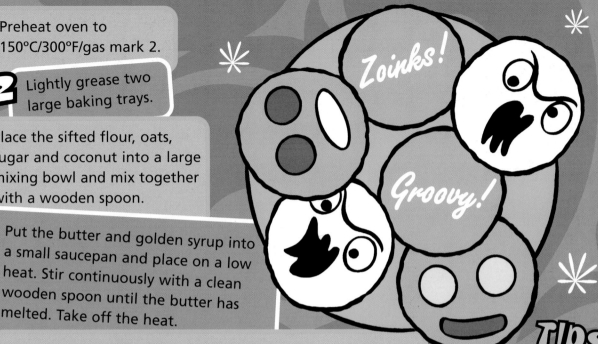

Zoinks!

Groovy!

Tips

* Personalize your Scooby Snacks by decorating with icing and sweets. Make smiley faces, or using an icing pipette, write messages for your friends!

* How do you like your cookies? Cook them a little less for chewier cookies, and a little longer for crisp cookies.

Like, what's the best thing to put in a Scooby Snack? Rot? Like, your teeth!

COWARDY CUSTARD AND JELLY

This is an easy but favourite dessert. Top with fruit, chopped nuts, sprinkles or sweets – whatever takes your fancy!

EQUIPMENT

mixing bowl

tablespoon

teaspoons

wooden spoon

saucepan

mug

serving bowls

INGREDIENTS   makes 4–6 servings

1 packet jelly

300ml milk

1 tablespoon sugar

2 teaspoons cornflour

1/2 teaspoon vanilla extract

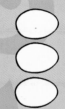
3 egg yolks

TIP

You will need to constantly stir the custard to prevent it from becoming lumpy. Or you could always buy custard powder or ready-made custard from the supermarket.

MAKING THE JELLY

1 Follow the directions on the back of the packet. You will need to make this in advance of the custard.

2 Spoon jelly out into bowls.

MAKING THE CUSTARD

1 Take a medium-sized saucepan with a heavy bottom, and put it on the heat. Place the cornflour and 2 tablespoons of the milk in the pan, and stir until the flour is dissolved.

2 Slowly add the rest of the milk and the sugar, stirring over a moderate heat until the sauce starts to thicken and bubble. Take off the heat.

3 Separate whites from egg yolks. Do this by cracking each egg in half and transferring the yolk from one shell to the other, letting the whites drip into a bowl below.

4 Put the jug to one side. In a small mixing bowl, beat the yolks.

5 Take about a cup of the mixture from the pot and pour into the bowl, beating well. Then pour the contents of the bowl into the saucepan.

6 Stir constantly, and bring the saucepan to the boil. Take off the heat.

7 Add vanilla extract and stir well.

8 Pour on top of the jelly. Sprinkle with toppings if you wish and eat straight away!

What's yellow and can see just as well in all directions?

Shaggy with his eyes shut tight!

SYRUPY PANCAKES

Nothing tastes better than hot pancakes. These mini-versions are fast to cook, and make a fab breakfast!

EQUIPMENT

mixing bowl

measuring jug

whisk

frying pan

wooden spoon

teaspoons

spatula

INGREDIENTS makes enough for 4 people

200g self-raising flour

25g caster sugar

125g fresh or frozen raspberries

250ml milk

maple syrup

sunflower oil

1 teaspoon baking powder

125g butter

1 teaspoon vanilla essence

2 eggs

1 Place the flour, baking powder, sugar and vanilla essence in a mixing bowl. Crack the eggs into the mixture and mix with a wooden spoon.

2 Gradually add the milk and whisk with a fork until the mixture is smooth.

3 Heat up a little of the oil in a large frying pan.

4 Heat for a couple of minutes, then pour spoonfuls of the pancake mixture into the pan. Don't make them too big – you should aim to fit three in the pan. Make sure you leave enough space between them too – you don't want the pancakes to join up into one monster pancake.

5 Cook until bubbles appear in the pancakes (about 1 minute) and flip over. The topside should be golden. Cook for a further minute, and flip to check if it is cooked. Remove and heap on a plate.

6 Continue making pancakes this way until you have used up the batter.

7 Divide and stack the pancakes on to four plates and butter them. Trickle a spoonful of maple syrup on to each stack and top with raspberries.

TIP

You can use other fruit as well – strawberries, blueberries or even chopped banana!

Hey, Scoob old pal – like, what sounds cold, but feels hot?

Ri ron't ro. Rot rounds rold, rut reels rot?

Like, chilli sauce, man!

CHOCOLATE BROWNIES

Chocolate brownies are one of the best Scooby Snacks around. You can use any type of chocolate or nuts – we have used dark chocolate and walnuts to add to their chewy texture.

EQUIPMENT

large mixing bowl

small mixing bowl

wooden spoon

fork

saucepan

shallow baking tray

greaseproof paper

INGREDIENTS

65g self-raising flour

175g soft brown sugar

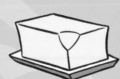

65g butter

2 eggs

50g plain chocolate

65g walnut pieces

TIP

Try this recipe with white or milk chocolate, peanuts, pecans or hazelnuts.

1 Pre-heat the oven to 180º/350ºF/gas mark 4.

2 Cut a square of greaseproof paper to fit the bottom of a shallow baking tray.

3 Put about 5 cm of tap water in a saucepan on the stove and simmer.

4 Chop up the butter into small squares and put in a small mixing bowl. Break up the chocolate and also place in the bowl. Carefully place the bowl inside the saucepan – you do not want to splash yourself with hot water. Stir the chocolate and butter with a wooden spoon until they have melted and mixed together. Take off the heat.

5 Take a large mixing bowl and break the eggs into it. Beat them with a fork. Using a wooden spoon, stir in the sugar, flour and walnuts. Then pour in the chocolate mixture and stir until the mixture is smooth.

6 Pour the mixture into the baking tray and cook in the oven for 30–35 minutes. Take the tin out of the oven and leave to cool. Cut into squares and devour!

What kind of dried fruit does the 10,000 volt ghost like best?

Currants!

47

LOOK OUT FOR THESE OTHER GREAT

SCOOBY-DOO!

TITLES FROM PUFFIN